MAZE

FOR KIDS

MAZE BOOK

SOCIAL MEDIA

- **f** /MySweetBooks1
- **𝕏** /MySweetBooks1
- **📷** /MySweetBooks1
- **P** /MySweetBooks

Email Us : mysweetbooks1@gmail.com

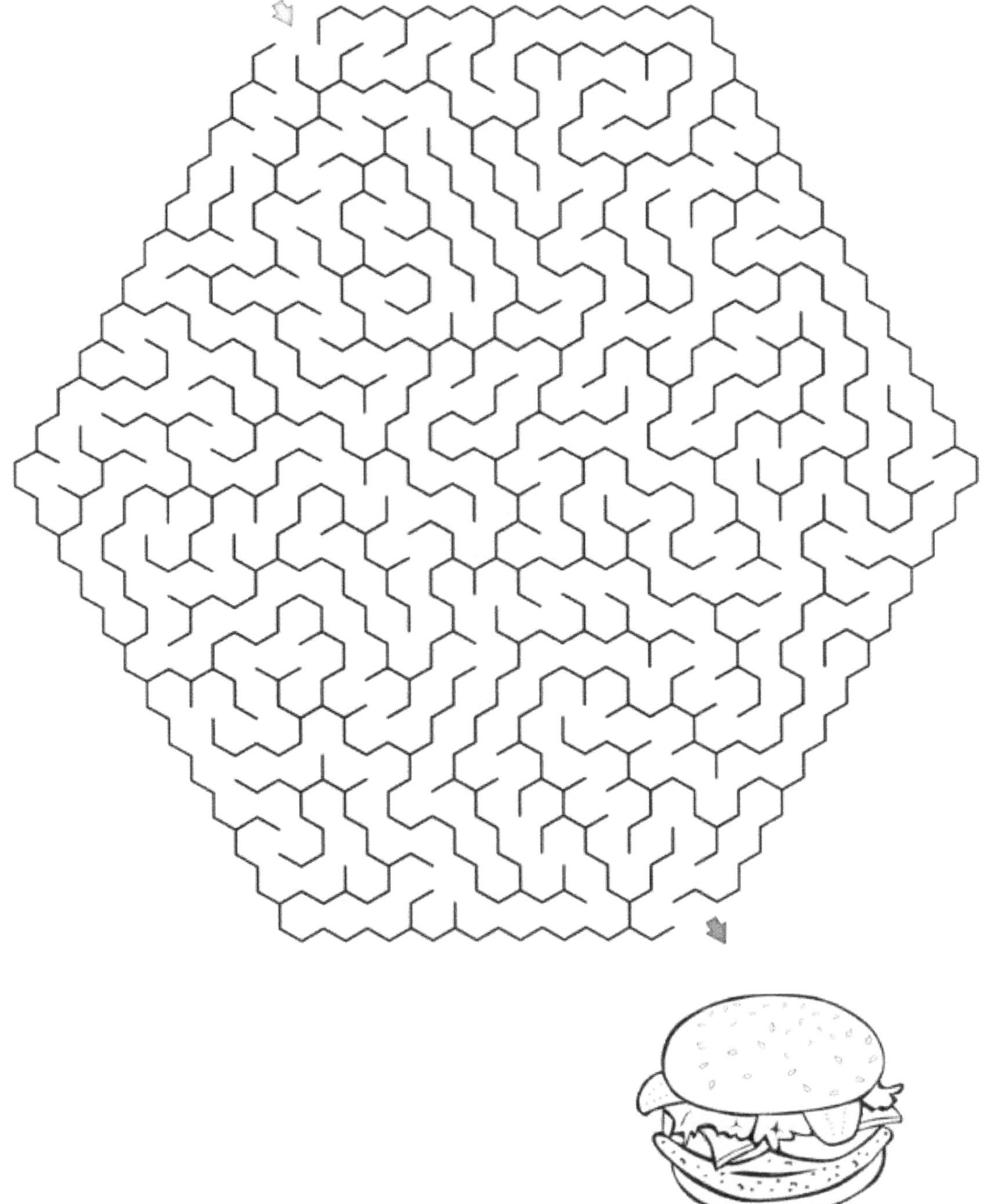

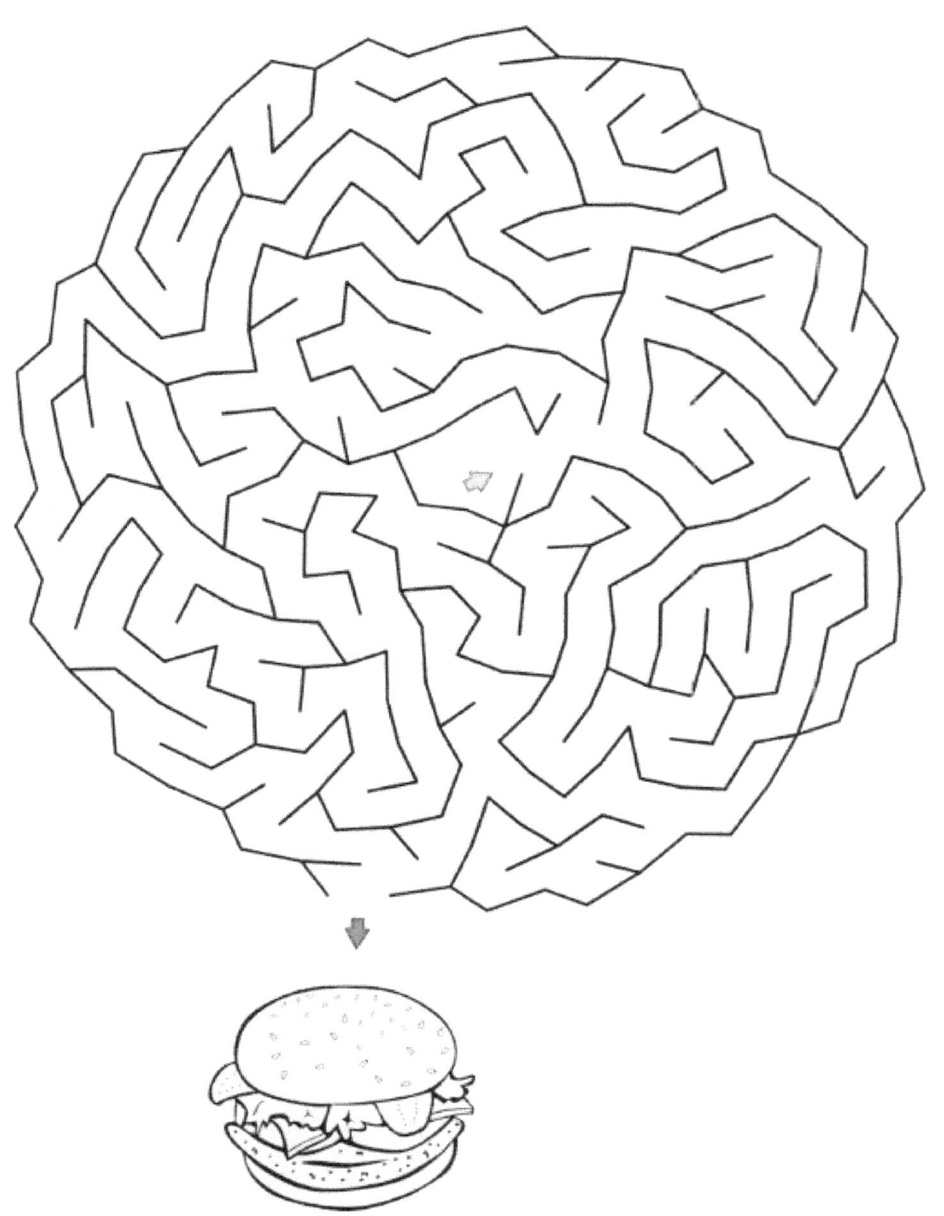

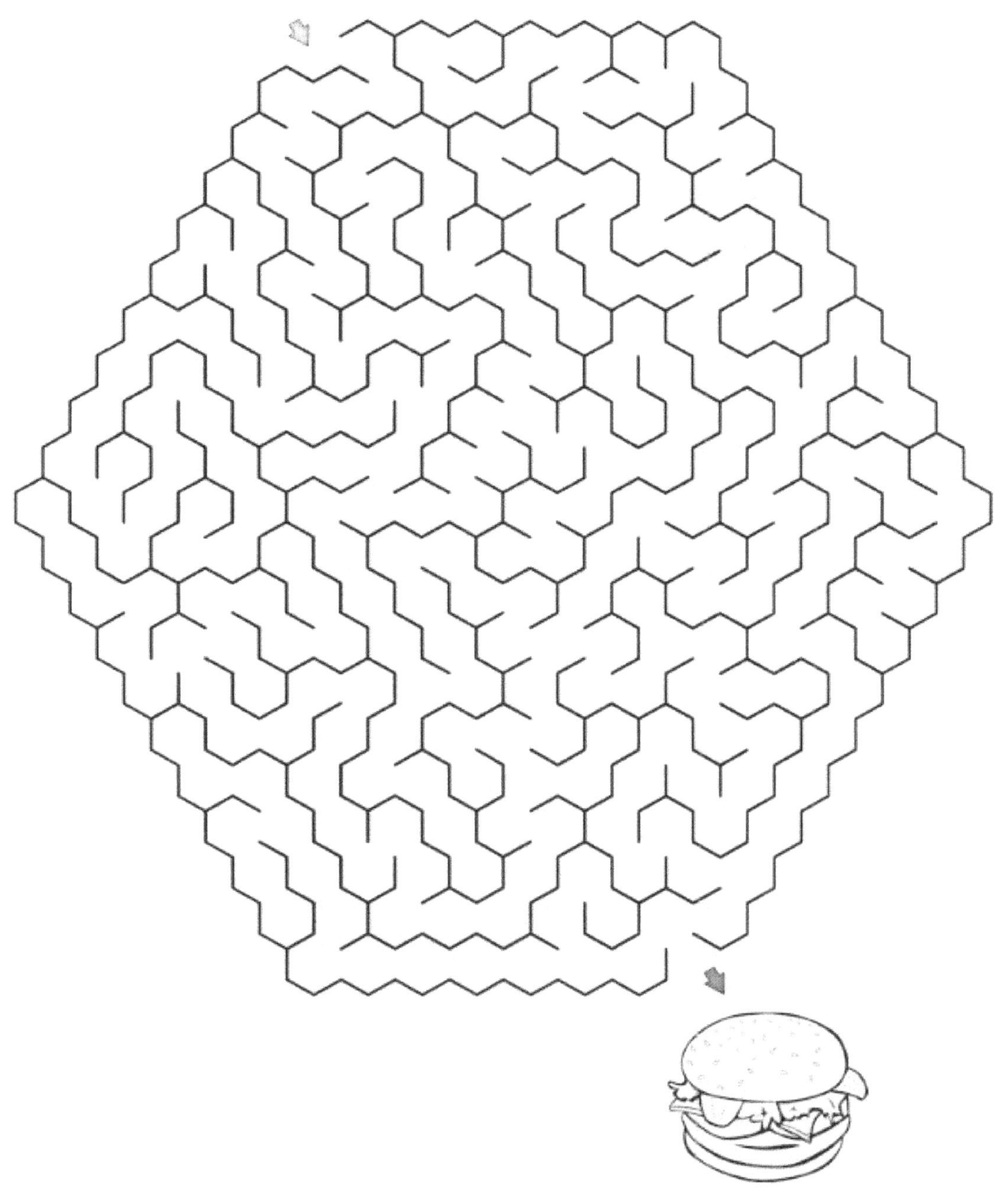

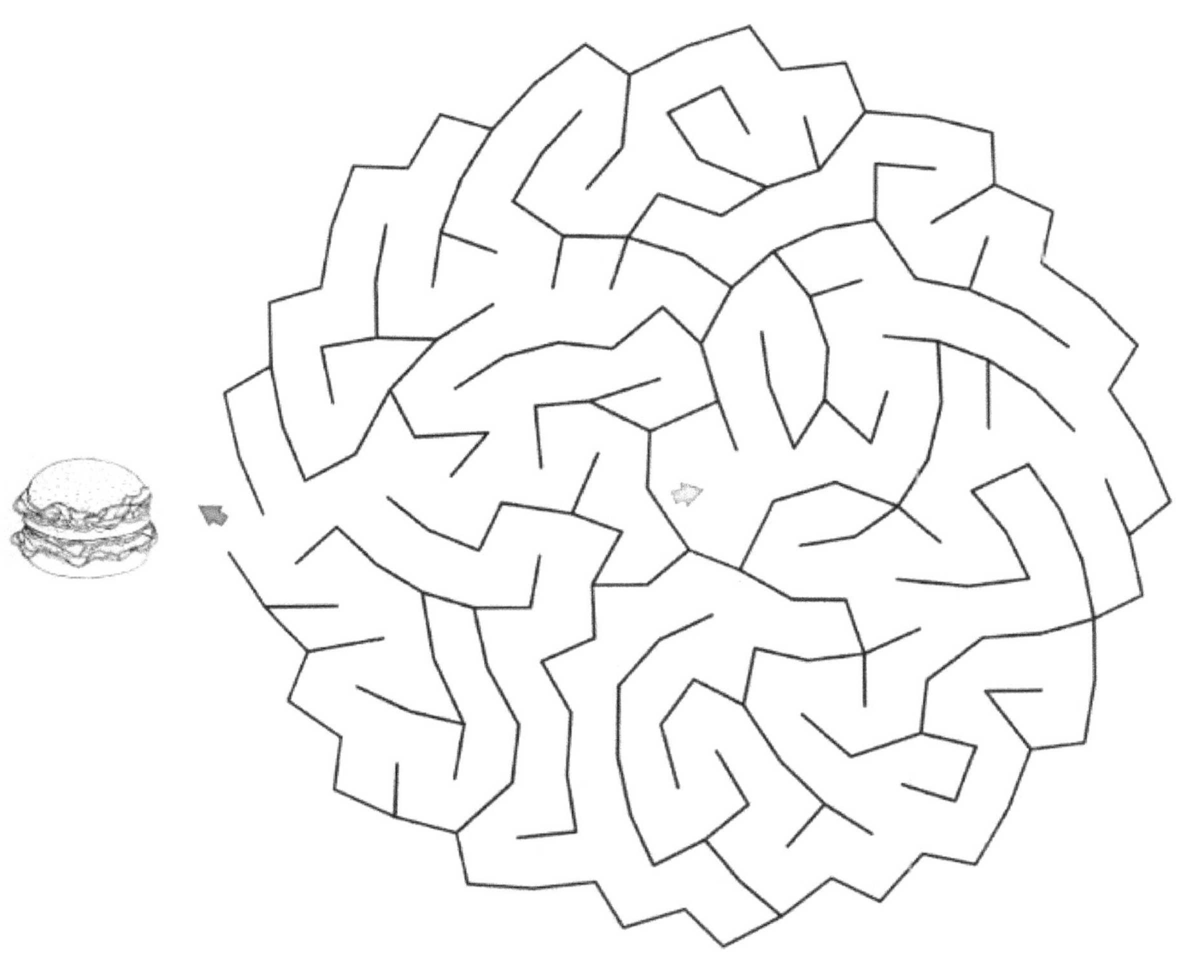

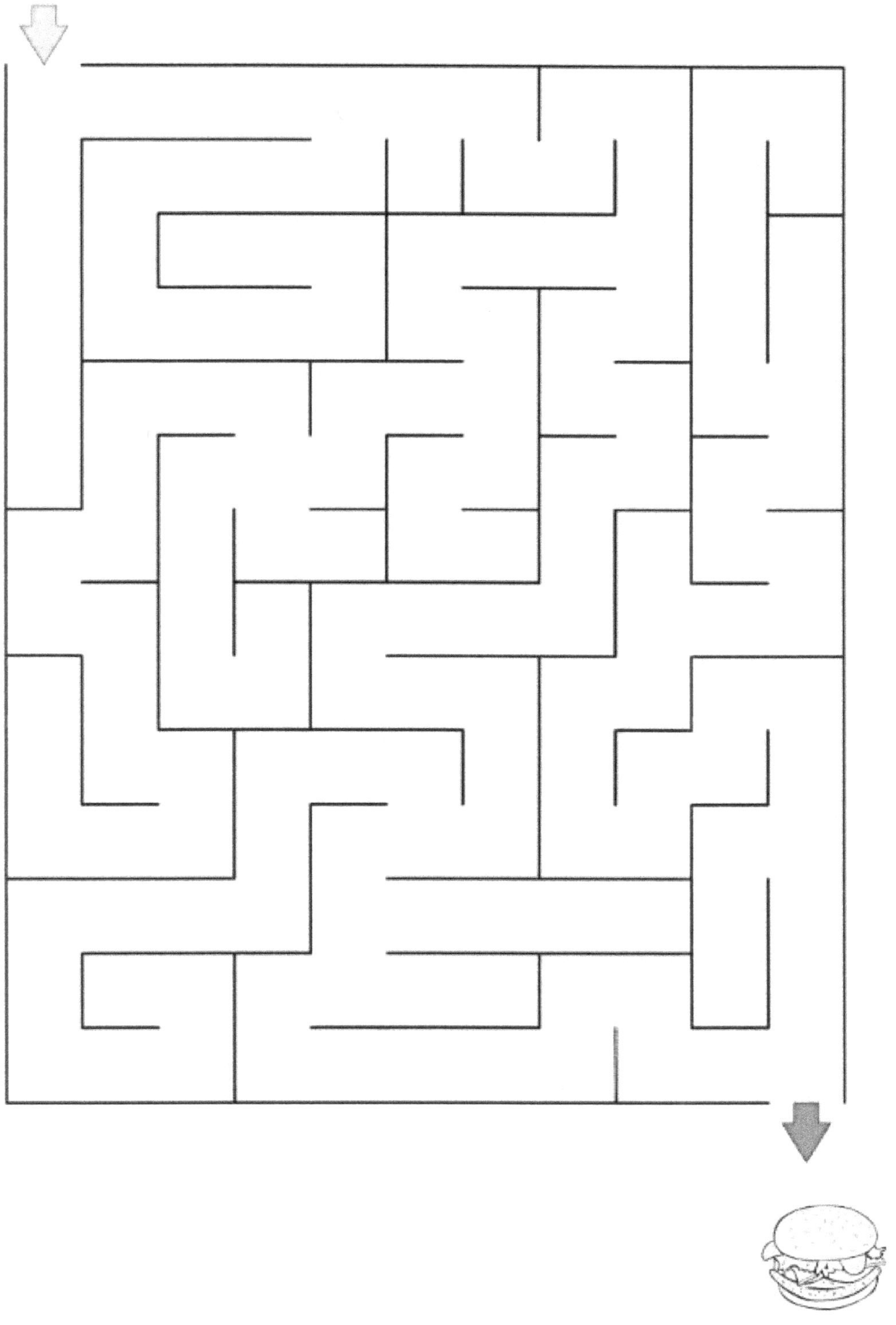

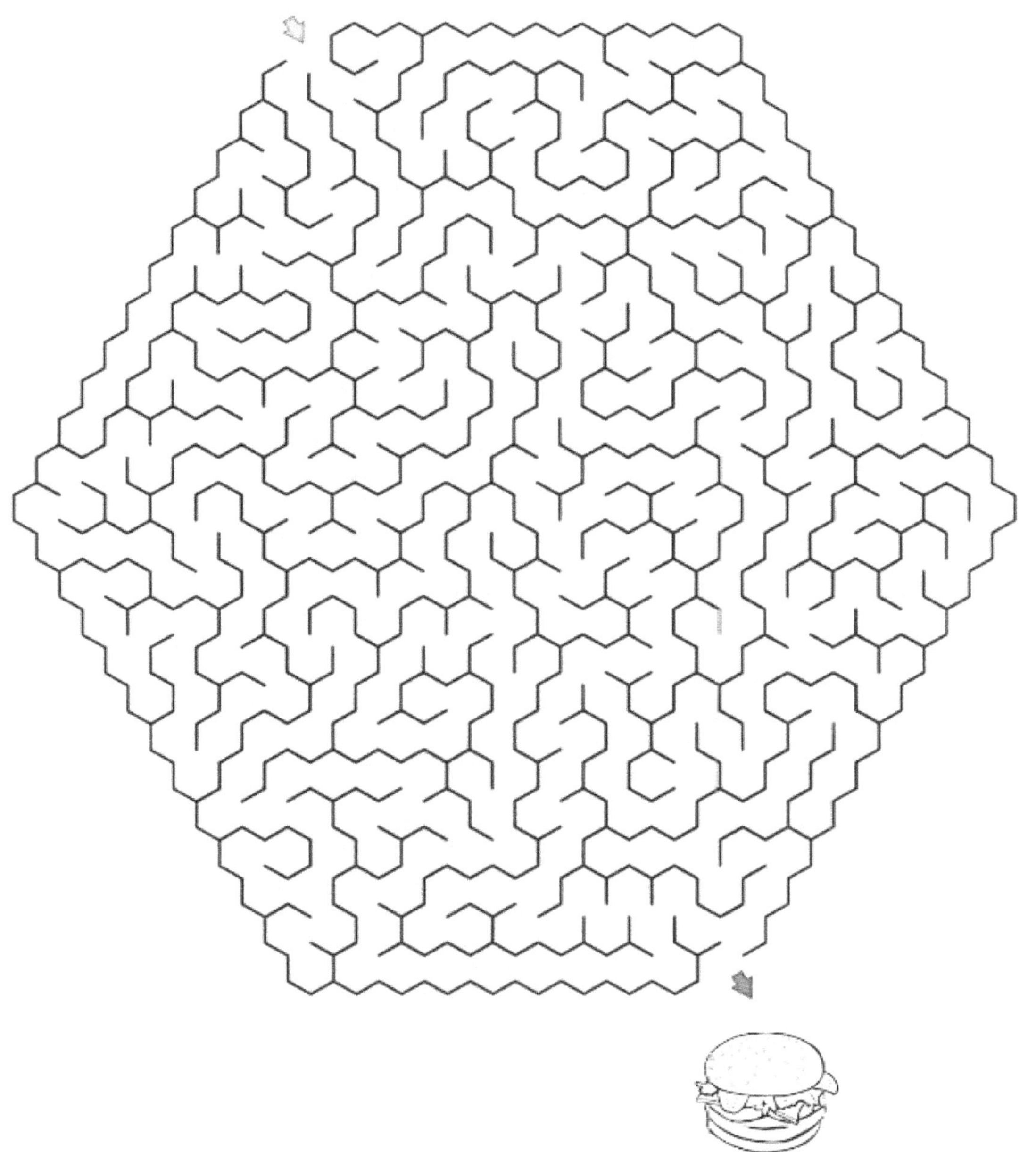

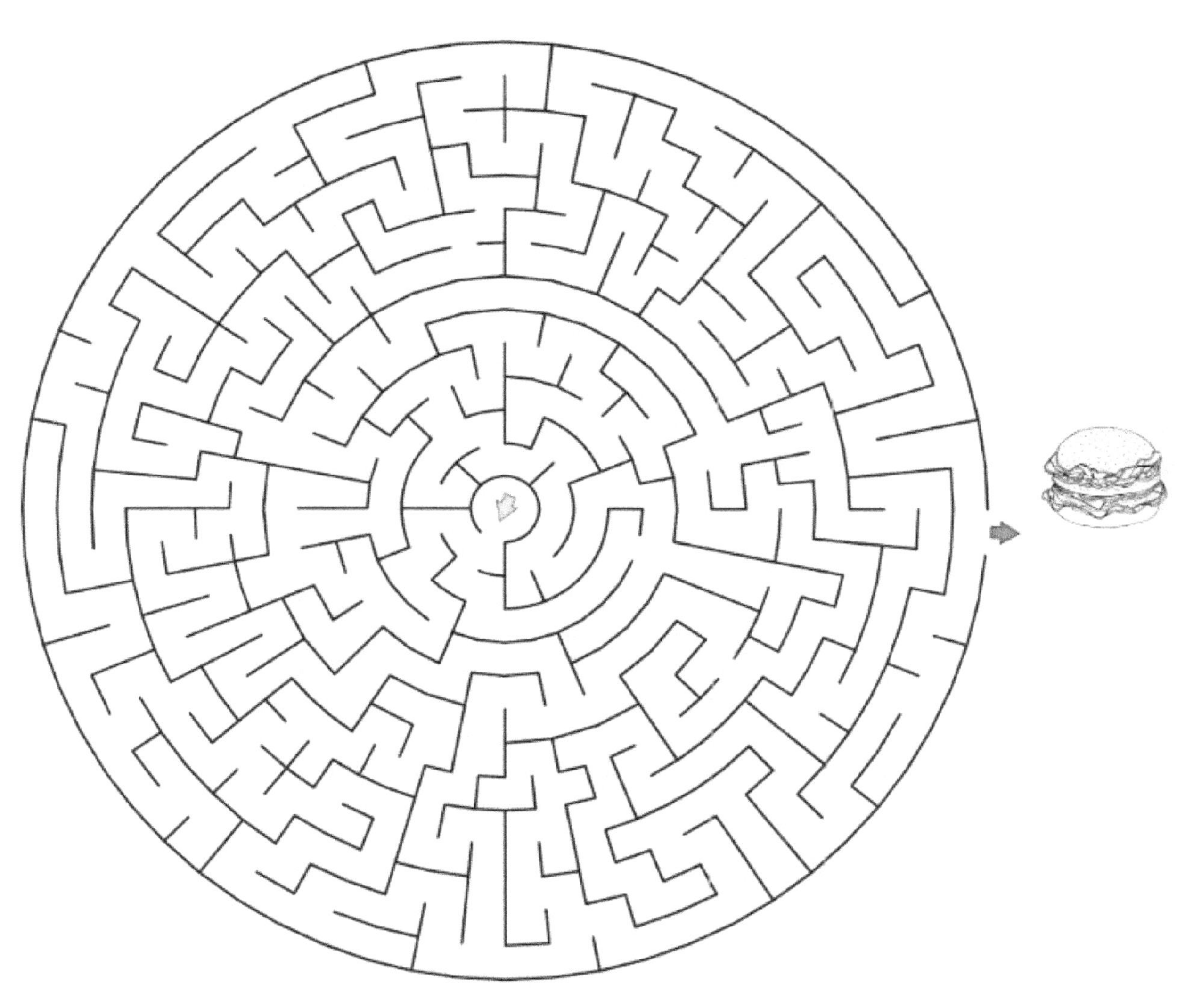

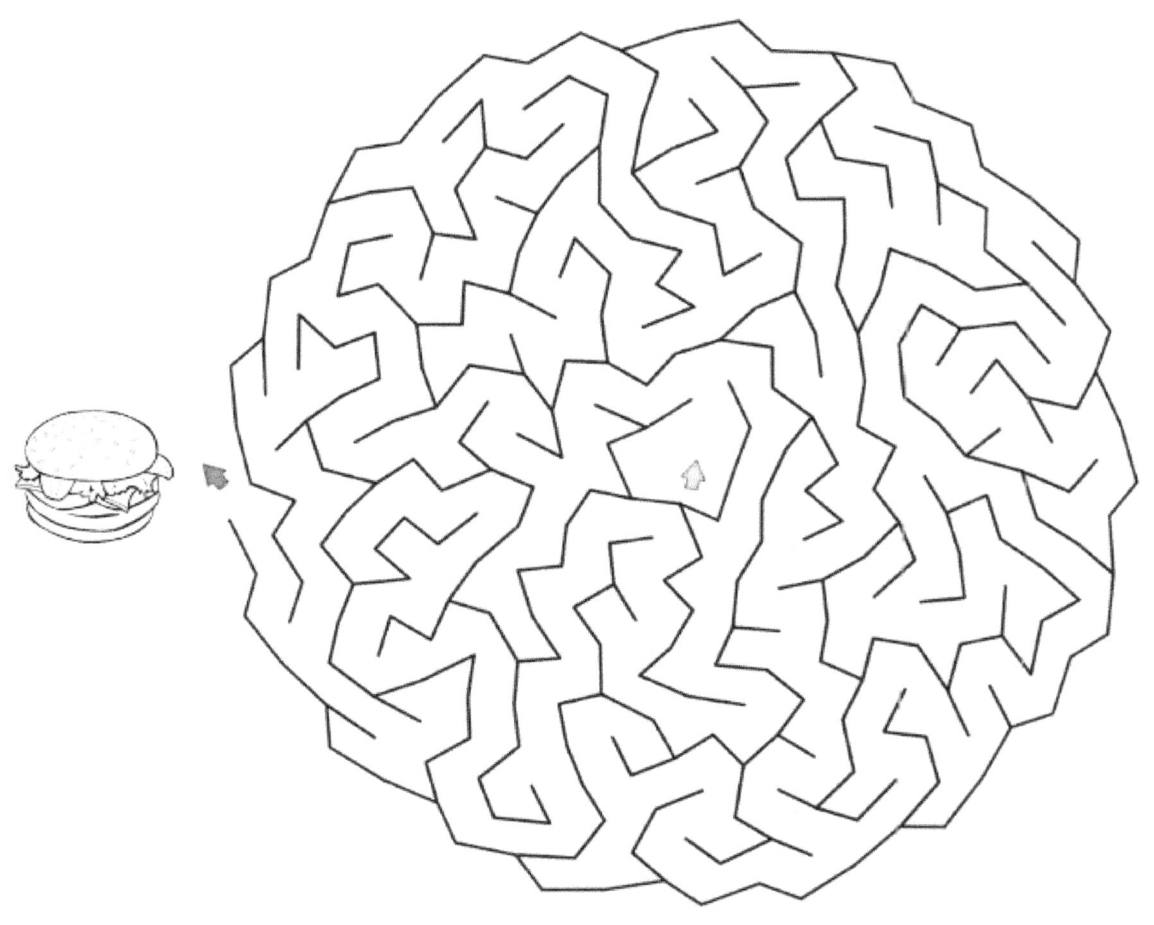

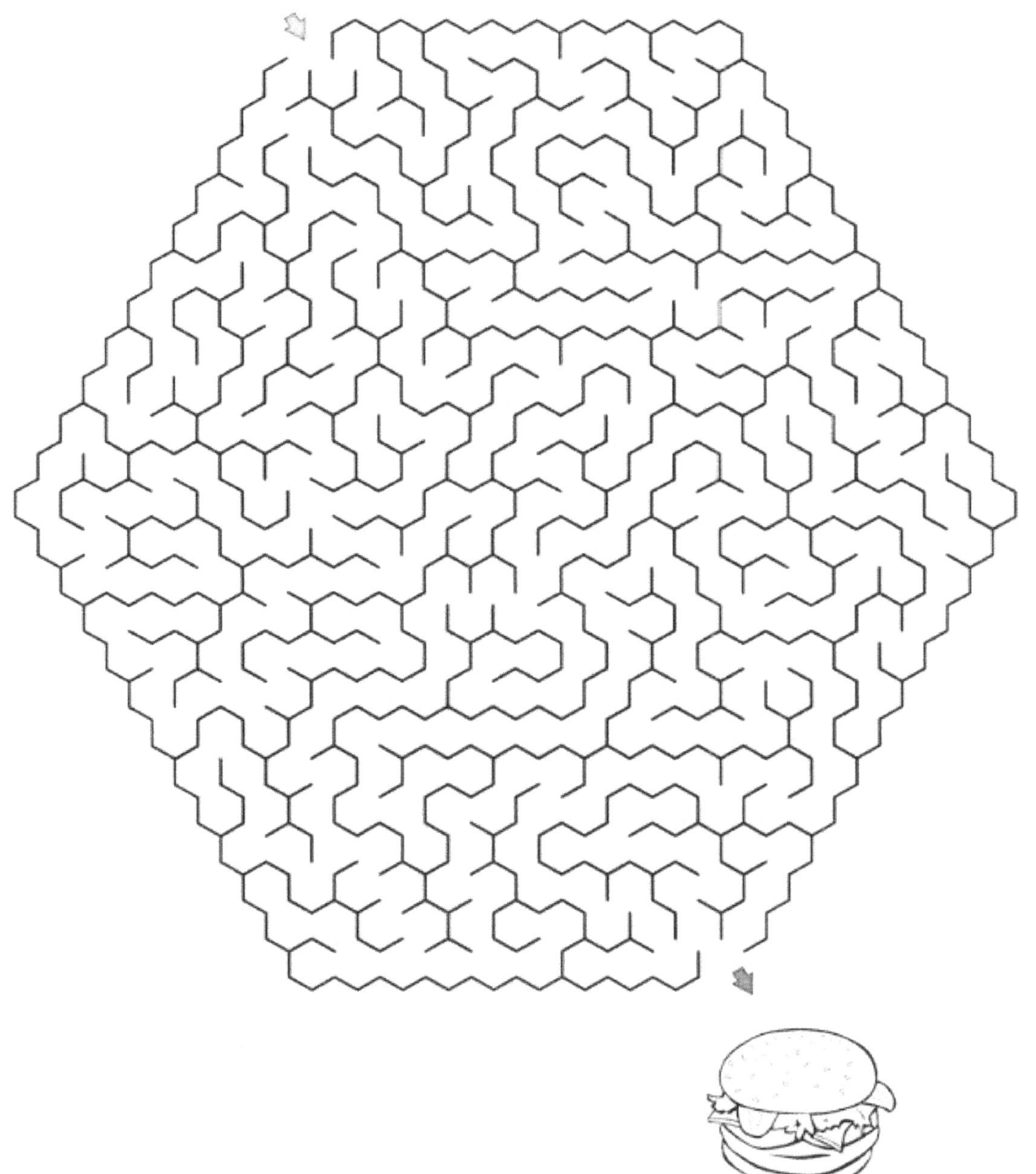

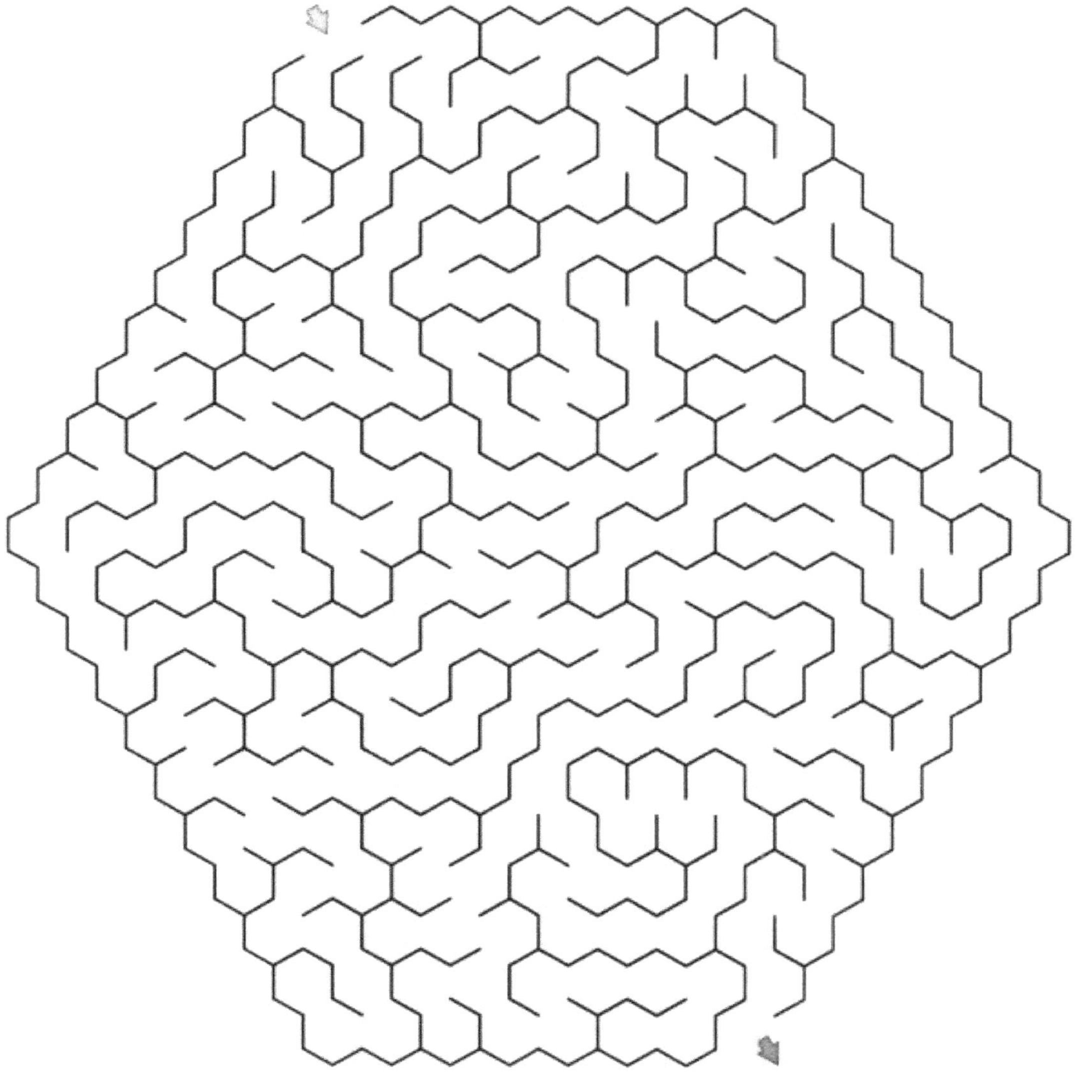

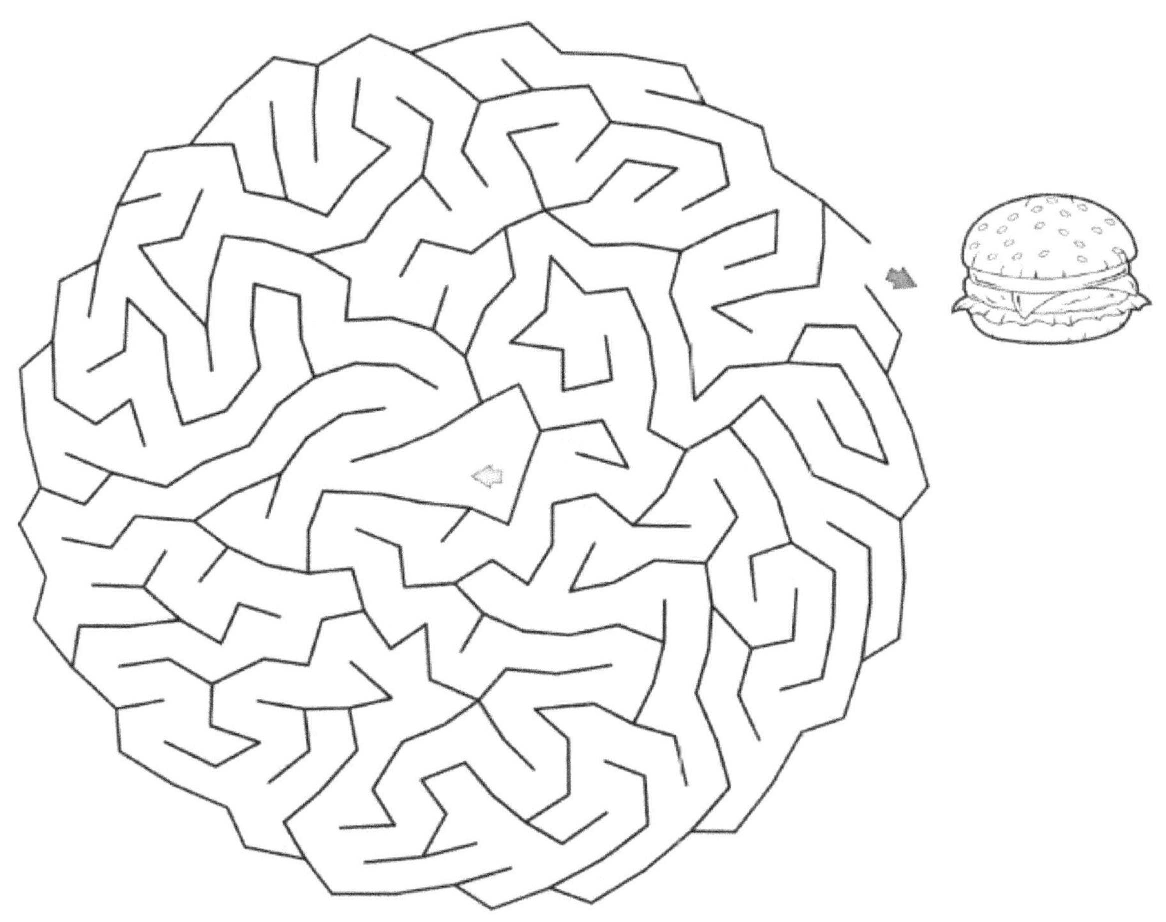

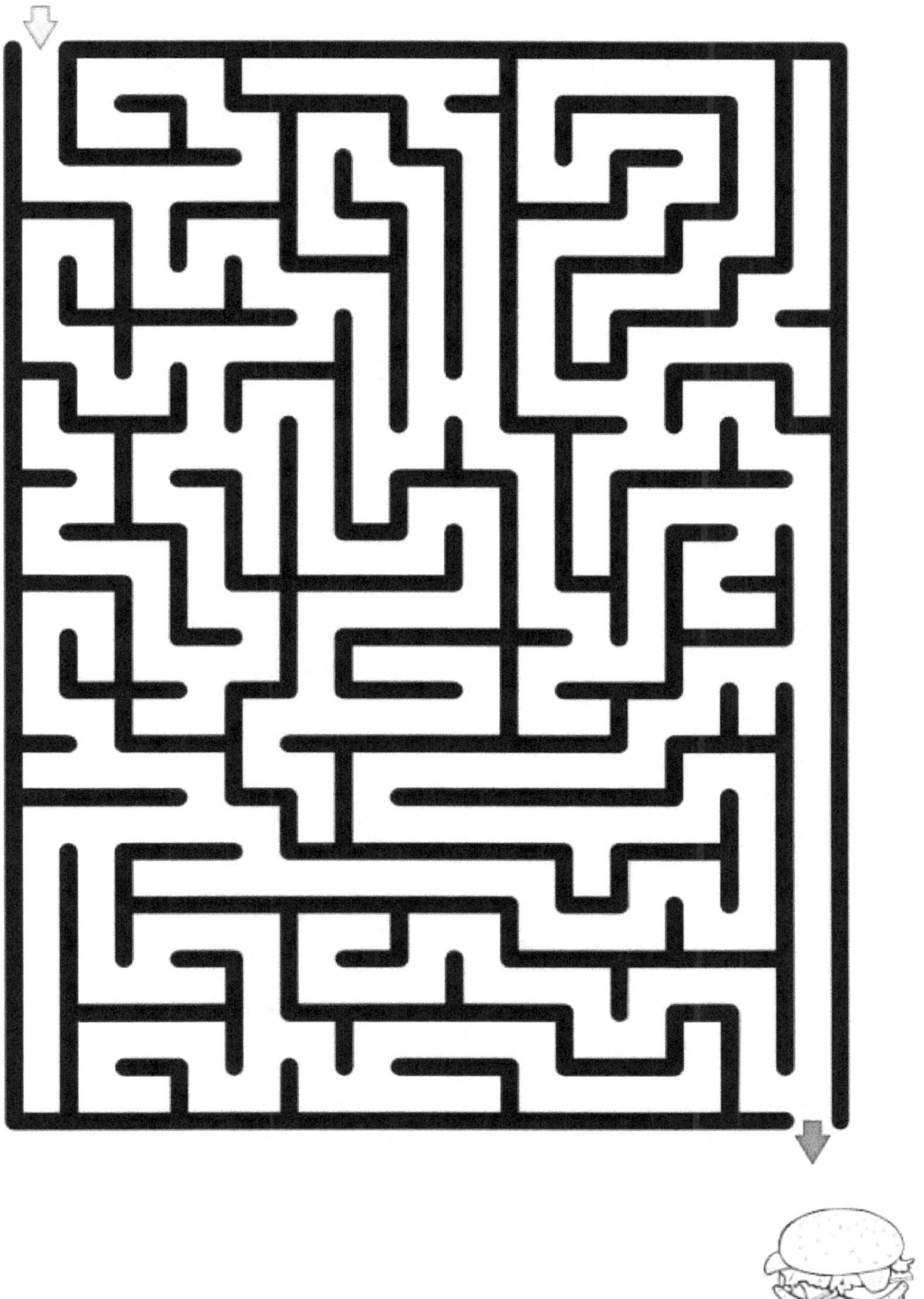